Thank Goodness for Little Girls

Cherishing Our Sweet Blessings from Above

PAINTINGS BY

Sandra Kuck

HARVEST HOUSE PUBLISHERS

EUGENE, OREGON

Thank Goodness for Little Girls

Copyright © 2004 by Harvest House Publishers
Eugene, Oregon 97402

ISBN 0-7369-1361-0

All works of art reproduced in this book are copyrighted by Sandra Kuck and may not be reproduced without the artist's permission. For more information regarding art prints featured in this book, please contact:

> V.F. Fine Arts, Inc.
> 1737 Stibbens St. #240B
> Houston, TX 77043
> 1.800.648.0405

Design and production by Garborg Design Works, Minneapolis, Minnesota

Harvest House Publishers has made every effort to trace the ownership of all poems and quotes. In the event of a question arising from the use of a poem or quote, we regret any error made and will be pleased to make the necessary correction in future editions of this book.

Scripture quotations are taken from the Holy Bible, New International Version®, Copyright © 1973, 1978, 1984 by the International Bible Society. Used by permission of Zondervan Publishing House.

Printed in Hong Kong

04 05 06 07 08 09 10 11/ NG / 10 9 8 7 6 5 4 3 2

A bright and sunny smiling face,

A mix of playfulness and grace,

A fun-loving and friendly way,

Of bringing joy to every day,

Her little hugs and kisses, too,

The way she works her wiles on you

And sets your heart all in a whirl …

These are the charms of a little girl.

AUTHOR UNKNOWN

4

A girl is a girl so frilly and sweet

You'd just like to hug her the moment you meet.

She's little pink ruffles and nylon and lace;

She's an innocent look on a little pink face;

…She's kittens and everything cuddly and nice—

Ah, sure 'n she's a bit of God's own paradise.

PHYLLIS C. MICHAEL

A lovely being, scarcely formed or moulded,
A rose with all its sweetest leaves yet folded.

LORD BYRON

A child is a curly, dimpled lunatic.

RALPH WALDO EMERSON

The flakes of snow covered her long fair hair, which fell in beautiful curls around her neck; but of that, of course, she never once now thought. From all the windows the candles were gleaming, and it smelt so deliciously of roast goose, for you know it was New Year's Eve; yes, of that she thought.

HANS CHRISTIAN ANDERSEN
THE LITTLE MATCH GIRL

How delicate the skin, how sweet the breath

of children!

EURIPIDES

Philosophers dispute whether it is the promise

of what she will be…that makes her attractive,

the undeveloped maidenhood, or the natural,

careless sweetness of childhood.

MARK TWAIN

What do little girls talk about?

What is their mystic theme?

Those still too young for puppy love,

Yet old enough to dream.

WILLIAM HERSCHELL

To an old father, nothing is more sweet

Than a daughter.

Boys are more spirited, but their ways

Are not so tender.

EURIPIDES

One of life's unsolved

mysteries is what young

girls giggle about.

E.C. McKenzie

Raise your daughter to know the Lord, and she will have a built-in chaperone.

AUTHOR UNKNOWN

Know what it is to be a child? It is to believe in love, to believe in loveliness, to believe in belief; it is to be so little that the elves can reach to whisper in your ear; it is to turn pumpkins into coaches, and mice into horses, lowness into loftiness, and nothing into everything, for each child has its fairy godmother in its own soul.

FRANCIS THOMPSON

13

'Tis true, your budding miss is very charming,

But shy and awkward at first coming out,

So much alarm'd, that she is quite alarming,

All Giggle, Blush; half Pertness, and half Pout;

And glancing at *Mamma*, for fear there's harm in

What you, she, it, or they, may be about,

The nursery still lisps out in all they utter—

Besides, they always smell of bread and butter.

LORD BYRON

Of all people, children are the most imaginative.

THOMAS MACAULAY

The child-heart is open to any and all avenues; an angel

would no more surprise it than a man. In dreams, in visions,

in visible and invisible ways, God can talk and reveal

Himself to a child; but this profound yet simple way is lost

forever—immediately we lose the open, childlike nature.

OSWALD CHAMBERS

I love it—I love it—the laugh of a child,

Now rippling and gentle, now merry and wild;

Ringing out on the air with its innocent gush,

Like the trill of a bird in the twilight's soft hush;

Floating up on the breeze like the tones of a bell,

Or the music that dwells in the heart of a shell;

Oh, the laugh of a child, so wild and so free,

Is the merriest sound in the world for me!

ISABEL ATHELWOOD

Give a little love to a child,

and you get a great deal back.

JOHN RUSKIN

I believe in little children as the most precious gift of Heaven to earth. I believe that they have immortal souls created in the image of God, coming forth from Him and to return to Him. I believe that in every child are infinite possibilities for good and evil and that the kind of influence with which she is surrounded in early childhood largely determines whether or not the budding life shall bloom in fragrance and beauty with the fruits thereof, a noble Godlike character.

RANDALL J. CONDON

Children know the grace of God
Better than most of us,
They see the world
The way the morning brings it
  back to them,
New and born and fresh
  and wonderful.

ARCHIBALD MACLEISH

"So I cut up the quilt," continued Margolotte, "and made from it a very well-shaped girl, which I stuffed with cotton-wadding. I will show you what a good job I did," and she went to a tall cupboard and threw open the doors.

Then back she came, lugging in her arms the Patchwork Girl, which she set upon the bench and propped up so that the figure would not tumble over.

Ojo examined this curious contrivance with wonder. The Patchwork Girl was taller than he, when she stood upright, and her body was plump and rounded because it had been so neatly stuffed with cotton. Margolotte had first made the girl's form from the patchwork quilt and then she had dressed it with a patchwork skirt and an apron with pockets in it—using the same gay material throughout. Upon the feet she had sewn a pair of red leather shoes with pointed toes. All the fingers and thumbs of the girl's hands had been carefully formed and stuffed and stitched at the edges, with gold plates at the ends to serve as finger-nails.

"She will have to work, when she comes to life," said Margolotte.

Frank L. Baum
The Patchwork Girl

*Every child born into
the world is a new
thought of God,
an ever-fresh and
radiant possibility.*

KATE DOUGLAS WIGGINS

*No joys on earth bring
greater pleasure than a little
girl to love and treasure.*

AUTHOR UNKNOWN

In alluding to myself as a Goose Girl,

I am using only the most modest of my

titles; for I am also a poultry-maid,

a tender of Belgian hares and rabbits,

and a shepherdess; but I particularly fancy

the role of Goose Girl, because it recalls

the German fairy tales of my early youth,

when I always yearned, but never hoped,

to be precisely what I now am.

KATE DOUGLAS WIGGIN
THE DIARY OF A GOOSE GIRL

Children are the

living messages we

send to a time we

will not see.

JOHN W. WHITEHEAD

Little girls are cute and small only to adults. To one another they are not cute. They are life-sized.

MARGARET ATWOOD

Now it was plain that the lady must be a real Princess, since she had been able to feel the three little peas through the twenty mattresses and twenty feather beds. None but a real Princess could have had such a delicate sense of feeling.

The Prince accordingly made her his wife; being now convinced that he had found a real Princess.

HANS CHRISTIAN ANDERSEN
THE REAL PRINCESS

The prime purpose of being four is to enjoy being four—of secondary importance is to prepare for being five.

JIM TRELEASE

There is a garden in every childhood, an enchanted place where colors are brighter, the air softer, and the morning more fragrant than ever again.

ELIZABETH LAWRENCE

She was perfectly quiet now, but not asleep—only soothed by sweet porridge and warmth into that wide-gazing calm which makes us older human beings, with our inward turmoil, feel a certain awe in the presence of a little child, such as we feel before some quiet majesty or beauty in the earth or sky—before a steady glowing planet, or a full-flowered eglantine, or the bending trees over a silent pathway.

GEORGE ELIOT

Mild and slow and young,

She moves about the room,

And stirs the summer dust

With her wide broom.

In the warm, lofted air,

Soft lips together pressed,

Soft wispy hair,

She stops to rest,

And stops to breathe

Amid the summer hum,

The great white lilac bloom

Scented with days to come.

JANET LEWIS

They are idols of hearts and of households;

They are angels of God in disguise;

His sunlight still sleeps in their tresses,

His glory still gleams in their eyes;

Those truants from home and from heaven

They have made me more manly and mild;

And I know now how Jesus could liken

The kingdom of God to a child.

CHARLES DICKINSON

A Princess she, though not by birth:

Her title's from above,

Her heritage the right of worth,

Her empire that of love.

FANNY E. NEWBERRY

Fairest flower, all flowers excelling,
　　Which in Eden's garden grew;
Flowers of Eve's embowered dwelling
　　Are, my fair one, types of you.
Mark, my Polly, how the roses
　　Emulate thy damask cheek;
How the bud its sweets discloses—
　　Buds thy opening bloom bespeak.

Lilies are, by plain direction,
　　Emblems of a double kind;
Emblems of thy fair complexion,
　　Emblems of thy fairer mind.
But, dear girl, both flowers and beauty
　　Blossom, fade, and die away;
Then pursue good sense and duty,
　　Evergreens that ne'er decay.

NATHANIEL COTTON

A toddling little girl is a center of common feeling which makes the most dissimilar people understand each other.

GEORGE ELIOT

You may chisel a boy into shape, as you would a rock, or hammer him into it, if he be of a better kind, as you would a piece of bronze. But you cannot hammer a girl into anything. She grows as a flower does.

JOHN RUSKIN

The soul is healed by being with children.

FYODOR DOSTOEVSKY

What feeling is so nice as a child's hand in yours? So small, so soft and warm—like a kitten huddling in the shelter of your clasp. A child's hand in yours what tenderness and power it arouses. You are instantly the very touchstone of wisdom and strength.

MARJORIE HOLMES

On a clear sunny morning in June two figures might be seen climbing the narrow mountain path; one, a tall strong-looking girl, the other a child whom she was leading by the hand, and whose little checks were so aglow with heat that the crimson color could be seen even through the dark, sunburnt skin. And this was hardly to be wondered at, for in spite of the hot June sun the child was clothed as if to keep off the bitterest frost. She did not look more than five years old, if as much, but what her natural figure was like, it would have been hard to say, for she had apparently two, if not three dresses, one above the other, and over these a thick red woollen shawl wound round about her, so that the little body presented a shapeless appearance, as, with its small feet shod in thick, nailed mountain-shoes, it slowly and laboriously plodded its way up in the heat.

JOHANNA SPYRI
Heidi

There is always one moment in childhood when the door opens and lets the future in.

GRAHAM GREENE

And the children held each other by the hand, kissed the roses, looked up at the clear sunshine, and spoke as though they really saw angels there. What lovely summer-days those were! How delightful to be out in the air, near the fresh rose-bushes, that seem as if they would never finish blossoming!

HANS CHRISTIAN ANDERSEN
THE SNOW QUEEN

It was a sorrowful parting between Bessy Conway and her father and

mother, and brothers and sisters, who had hitherto been her world. It was

to her something like launching into the regions of air far beyond mortal

ken, and as she sobbed out her last farewell on her mother's shoulder,

she thought she could not live so far away from home, and friends, and

parents. And yet their parting was not so heart-rending as many others

they saw around them. It was brightened by hope, cheering hope, for

Bessy had a good home to come back to, in case she did not like

America, and she went with the special condition that, in any case,

she would return in the course of a few years, if God spared her life.

MARY ANNE SADLIER
BESSY CONWAY

A child's eyes! Those clear wells
of undefiled thought! What on
earth can be more beautiful? Full
of hope, love, and curiosity, they
meet your own. In prayer, how
earnest! In joy, how sparkling! In
sympathy, how tender!

CAROLINE NORTON

And whoever welcomes

a little child like this in

my name welcomes me.

THE BOOK OF MATTHEW

Sandra Kuck
©2000

Once Molly paused, inspecting a small cream-cake in her hand with a grave air.

"What is it, dear? What are you thinking?" asked Miss Prue, to whom the child was always a whole page of fun and epigram.

"I was thinking, ma'am, how does this froth get inside the cake?"

"Molly, Molly! You are too curious," said her sister.

But now an idea suddenly struck the child, rippling and dimpling over her bright face like a breeze over a little lake.

"Oh, I know!" she cried, "I know! You just churn the cream, and then pour the dough around it, of course!" which lucid explanation seemed perfectly satisfactory to herself at any rate.

Fanny E. Newberry
Sara, A Princess

*A*nd once when someone gave Bessie Bell a little round

red apple she caught her breath very quickly and her little

heart jumped and then thumped very loudly (that is the

way it seemed to her) and she remembered: Little apple

trees all just alike, and little apple trees in rows all just alike

on top of those and again on top of those until they came to

a great row of big round red apples on top of all.

MARTHA YOUNG
SOMEBODY'S LITTLE GIRL